FORGIVENESS
&
CONFESSION

FORGIVENESS & CONFESSION

THE KEYS TO RENEWAL

By

Alvin N. Rogness

AUGSBURG PUBLISHING HOUSE

Minneapolis   Minnesota

FORGIVENESS AND CONFESSION
The Keys to Renewal
Copyright © 1970 by Augsburg Publishing House
All rights reserved
Library of Congress Catalog Card No. 75-121960

Manufactured in the United States of America

To the members and staff of
the Lutheran World Federation
Commission on Worship and
Spiritual Life whose reflections
are mirrored in these chapters.

Contents

Preface

As a member of the Commission on Worship and Spiritual Life of the Lutheran World Federation I have participated in the effort to explore what the church needs to emphasize so that the life of the congregations may reflect the work of the Holy Spirit in our day. Our Commission has not concentrated on the corporate structures of modern life: rather it has turned its attention to man himself and to the effects which the increased complexities of our day have had on him. We have sought to reassess that about the Gospel and about man which remain essentially unchanged.

It appeared evident almost from the start

that the church's task in every age must be to exalt Christ and His redeeming work, and that therefore it would seem right to focus on the forgiveness of sins and the confession of sins as keys to a renewal of the life of the congregation. We have explored the subject from the viewpoints of many disciplines—theological, psychological, philosophical, sociological—and with the help of specialists in each area.

This little book is an attempt to summarize the Commission's findings in language that is not technical, but that may be read and discussed by reflective congregation members.

ALVIN N. ROGNESS

Forgiveness is both the gateway to God and the climate of the life with God

1

Forgiveness -
a Constant for All Times

Is there a way of life that distinguishes the Christian? Does he have an inner life which is different? Does he have insights and resources which are unique? In his relation to the world and to his fellow men, is he different from other men?

Jesus said, "Behold, I make all things new." He told Nicodemus, "You must be born anew." He announced the Kingdom, and said, "The Kingdom of God is in the midst of you." He declared that in coming to God we were indeed coming from death to life. All through the centuries the followers of Jesus have believed that they were captured by something utterly new. They were, in Peter's words, a peculiar people.

What above all else describes this newness of life? New strength? New moral insights? New courage? New hope? New love?

This newness focuses on the forgiveness of sins. Man is loved of God; he is forgiven by God! Forgiveness is both the gateway to God and the climate of the life with God. He came from God; he returns to God. This is the destined biography of man. How does he return to God, and upon returning, how does he live with God, and how does he live with his fellow men? This is our concern.

During the Reformation the towering question was, "How does a man return to God?" In our day for vast numbers of men the question is, "Is there a God to whom a man may return?" God is no longer taken for granted. In the past four centuries the ingenuity of man to uncover the secrets of the physical world has tended to edge God out to the borders of life. He no longer is in the center. For many he has disappeared altogether.

With God gone, man is at a loss for a center. What is existence about? What meaning does it have? Is survival its only goal?

And is survival alone a goal meaningful enough to arouse the noblest aspirations of man?

These wider anxieties have penetrated the life of the church itself. In addressing itself to the state of the church, its worship and spiritual life, the commission has been sensitive to the erosion that the secular culture has had on the church's traditional and age-old articles of faith. To ignore this would be for the church to speak to itself and not to the world. Nor would it speak authentically even to itself.

There are certain assumptions which the church can neither escape nor surrender. It has an unchanging message about God, the God who is the same yesterday, today, and forever. And despite the effect of environment on man, man too is much the same, whether he rides on the back of a donkey or flies through the air in a jetliner. There are constants. God and man must come together, live together, and approach the management of the earth together—much the same in the twentieth century as in the first.

The world has undergone volcanic changes, especially in the last two centuries. And

change may only increase. The glad news of
life with God through forgiveness in Jesus
Christ must be proclaimed as the church's
unique message, change or no change. But if
the church is to be faithful in its proclama-
tion, it must be sensitive to the modern con-
text, the frame, in which man now lives.

Try as he will,
man cannot escape
the imperative of
responsibility
and therefore
the sense
of guilt.

2

The Man of Today

The last one hundred and fifty years have witnessed a veritable explosion in technological knowledge. Century after century life had remained essentially the same. For thousands of years in transportation the fleetest conveyance was a horse on a dry track traveling about thirty-five miles an hour. Then came the steam engine, and today we fly to the moon at incredible speed. In this century alone we have witnessed the advent of the airplane, radio, television, electronics, atomic energy, the computer. Suddenly nature is yielding her secrets. Scientists predict that the next ten years will see greater changes than the last fifty.

It is not strange that man oscillates between pride and bewilderment. What has the mind of man wrought! He can travel faster, see farther, and hear more than ever before. With new sources of power he can produce goods a hundredfold in variety. He has been incredibly successful.

But his success is toward limited, and often questionable, goals. This fact now haunts him. At the very moment when he ought to be elated over his triumphs and have unlimited hope for the future, man finds himself wondering, in fact, often despairing. When in the early days of the telephone, Thoreau of Walden Pond was informed that people of Boston had spoken to the people of Texas, he responded with the question, "But did the people of Boston have anything to say to the people of Texas?" There are goals other than power and speed, in fact, goals that power and speed may jeopardize.

Not only knowledge has been exploding. Population, too, has spiraled. The combination of the two has loosened colossal, impersonal forces which threaten to destroy man. What can one man do in the face of these huge movements? Even the most ingenious of the scientists and the boldest of social planners face the future with something less than courage. Have we opened Pandora's box, and must we stand by to await the holocaust?

Although medical science has lengthened life to where the thought of death seems no longer the ever-present private issue of years ago, the fear of catastrophe lurks in the mind of modern man—and with catastrophe, death. A boy of twelve asked, "What chance do my friends and I have of living out a normal lifetime?" The prospect of death always raises the question of the ultimate purpose of life. Modern man's uneasiness about goals for life may not be unrelated to the subdued but real thought of death.

Strangely enough, modern man is harassed by feelings of guilt. Eloquent evidence of this is to be found in writers of fiction and drama as well as in the case histories of psychiatry. At the very moment when former canons of right and wrong are abandoned and society has become "permissive," the sense of guilt has become an almost universal symptom of man's plight. The strain on interpersonal relationships in a complex society and the awareness of the chasm between what the society

of man ought to be and what it is may ac-
count for this. In this gap between what life
ought to be and what it is lie anxiety, name-
less fears, broken dreams—all of which produce the feelings of guilt. Try as he will, man
cannot escape the imperative of responsibility, and therefore the sense of guilt.

To be sure, there are important social and
philosophical tendencies that focus attention
away from the idea of individual responsibility. Both the Marxist substitution of alienation for guilt and the Freudian diagnosis of
inner conflicts as the cause of neurosis and its
guilty feelings militate against the sense of
personal responsibility. Similarly, studies in
sociology and psychology have tended to lo-
cate man's trouble in adverse environmental
conditions, and thus to release man from responsibility. But instinctively man knows that
he is more than a blob of chemistry, more
than a bit of cosmic debris driven helplessly
on by forces beyond all control. He has the
gift of choice. He can make decisions. And he
is the kind of creature in which guilt may
dwell.

It is commonplace to say of modern man
that he has lost God. The dimension of tran-

scendence is gone. God threatens him no
longer; it is his world that now overwhelms
him. Once it was God who sent the rain and
the sun; it was God who favored an army
with victory; it was God who returned a man
to health; it was God who punished him in
his disobedience and rewarded him in his
faithfulness.

It cannot be denied that God has drifted
off to the edges of man's daily life and per-
haps for many has disappeared altogether.
But not without man's grief. An emptiness
and loneliness have overtaken modern man.
A vacuum yawns before him. He has longings
and yearnings for something—he knows not
what—something that will give meaning and
completeness to life. This something is God.
It would be reassuring to have a God who
acts in history, who puts limits to man's self-
destruction, who stands by to help manage
this planet. Left alone, man yields to panic or
paralysis, or both. He can stand to be the co-
pilot, but he cannot stand to be the pilot; he
can stand to be a son of God, but he cannot
stand to be on the throne.

With God gone, the category of authority
disappears. Man no longer says, "We must

obey God rather than man," nor does he say "How then can I do this great wickedness, and sin against God?" He is at sea; he finds no certain focus for authority. He may respect social contract, but only as a *modus vivendi* for getting along with his fellow men. He may adopt the democratic principle that the voice of the people is the voice of God, but ultimately this too fails as a focus for authority. He is left alone without a sovereign and without law, or becomes the victim of all sorts of fraudulent claimants for authority. Man, who was made for obedience, finds no one to obey. He is left to create moral order in a universe that has no transcendent basis for order. He cries for a judge, but the bench is empty.

Finally, hope is gone. He tries to generate courage for the future by an inventory of his own achievements. Spectacular as they are in the field of technology, his triumphs gives him no hope. He is left alone to manage the machine, which threatens to be unmanageable. He sees looming up before him the angry clouds of the hurricane, the mammoth problems of his time. And behind the clouds there is no one to lean on, no everlasting arms in which to rest, no power greater than his own to come to the rescue. Lonely man goes his lonely way to a vast and lonely grave.

This is modern man—without God. He may strut in bravado. He may distract himself with endless analyses. He may plunge headlong toward his limited goals. He may capitulate into despair and nihilism. But lurking underneath the surface of his consciousness is a great sadness, a homesickness. He wants to find a home in this universe. He may not use the words of Job, "Oh, that I knew where I might find Him," but the cry is there. Man wants God.

Man, if he is to have dignity or worth at all,

must be given the honor of being judged.

If he is neither good nor bad, neither justified nor condemned, he is no longer man!

3

The Confusion About Sin

There was a day when the word *sin* was as universal as the word *man*. Man was a fallen man, and therefore a sinful man. He disobeyed God; he rebelled against God. This was his sin.

With the advent of the disciplines of psychology and sociology, the word sin has been replaced by a number of other terms, none of which takes seriously the fact of God. In fact, since these disciplines employ scientific methods, they cannot postulate the presence of a divine being. They, as other scientific disciplines, must be restricted to phenomena that can be observed and measured.

Not only does God disappear from the field

of observation, but it has been difficult for these studies to allow for man's free will. Man has become a phenomenon completely conditioned by heredity and environment and by biochemical factors. Since he is not a self-determining creature, he therefore cannot be held responsible for what he is or what he becomes. And if he cannot be held responsible, there is no occasion for him to be given either blame or credit. He needs no forgiveness, because he cannot help doing what he does or being what he is. He has no more freedom than the chemical elements in the test tube. The moment the unpredictable and radical factor of freedom of the will is allowed, the whole enterprise threatens to be unscientific, beyond that which can be readily observed and measured.

Man's behavior can then no longer be called good or evil. His patterns of behavior may be "judged" to be of service to certain ends or objectives which the group approves, or they may be "judged" hostile to these ends. But the words good and evil disappear from the vocabulary of the scientist, or, if they are retained, they lose their original meaning.

This determinism is man's melancholy. It is the loss of his essential humanity. He had hoped to be the manager; now he is the managed one. He had aspired to be the actor; now he is an object acted upon by a myriad of forces. He not only has lost God; he has lost himself. He has lost the dignity of being a sinner.

But man does not give up this dignity easily. Responsibility does not die without a struggle, and guilt hovers near his consciousness. He needs to be judged; he cries for a verdict. In Arthur Miller's play *After the Fall*, Qunitus, the lawyer whose life is falling apart, says in one of the opening lines that he had thought of life as a case at law. When he was young, he tried to prove how strong and smart he was; later, what a good lover; then, what a good father; finally, when he was old, how mighty and wise. But, he goes on to say, he expected to be judged, to be justified or condemned—he expected some verdict, in any event. He states that one day he looked up and the bench was empty, there was no judge in sight. And without a judge, life became an endless conversation with himself, a pointless litigation of existence before an empty bench—which is despair.

Man, if he is to have dignity or worth at all, must be given the honor of being judged. If he is neither good nor bad, neither justified nor condemned, he is no longer man!

Even if sin does not reappear as offense against God, it comes to the surface in man's relation with his fellow men. He recognizes that he has wronged or hurt his brother, and that he needs reconciliation (forgiveness) if things are to be right again. This awareness is to be found first in his interrelations in family or tribe; but the more socially sensitive man becomes, the wider does this need for reconciliation become. This recognition always involves awareness of the hurt (confession) and the desire for healing (forgiveness). Whether religious language is used or not, this process of reconciliation between man and man is a symbol or type of the relation between God and man.

His offense may be not only against an individual, but against the group. His behavior separates or estranges him from the group—the state, for instance—and he needs restoration to the group, again through acknowledgment of offense, and acceptance by the group.

In our day we witness a new awareness of man's offense against mankind itself. Our nationalisms give way to a growing internationalism. The welfare of peoples the world over is increasingly interlocked. The magnificent statement on human rights approved by the United Nations is evidence of this dimension of humanitarianism. What happens to people in Biafra or in Hong Kong or Vietnam is my responsibility, for the peoples everywhere are my brothers.

With every increased sensitivity in the area of interhuman relations there is the element of guilt. But this is guilt over against man and not over against God. It is a horizontal phenomenon, not a vertical one. Man yearns for peace with his fellow men, not with God.

The tragedy of man is that reconciliation with his fellow men is always partial, even at best. He needs a forgiveness in the center of his being, and from the heart of the universe. He needs to understand that his offenses against his fellow men, in the final analysis, are a sin against the God who gave life to all men. His estrangement is not merely a break between him and his brothers, nor an estrangement within himself. It is an alienation from him who is his God and Savior. Not until he is made whole in God will he know peace and freedom.

If he is other than
a person,

then God is
at best
an idea
for vain speculation

4

The God to Whom Man Cries

A person cries to a Person. God may be infinitely more than a Person, but he must be at least "as much as" a Person if we are to have any communication with him. If God is described as "the ground of being" or "the origin of all things" or "the first principle," we in effect put him beyond reach of man and his prayers. Unless he is endowed with the qualities that describe *personhood*—holiness, righteousness, judgment, salvation—he remains but an abstraction. Neither the philosopher nor the cab driver can pray to "the primeval force of the universe."

It is only as God is a Person with a will that he becomes of significance to the human race. If he is other than a Person, then God is at best but an idea for vain speculation. He cannot enter the orbit of man's experience. He is totally irrelevant to man's existence. There can be neither faith nor apostasy.

When in the wake of science man was forced to surrender the comfortable three-story universe, he found it increasingly difficult to include a personal God in his understanding of the universe. The universe seemed to be a vast machine, complex and relentless in its orderliness. There might be room for a Creator God at the start, but once the machine had been created, there was no room for the intervention or penetration of God. If he existed at all, he was as helpless as we to reverse or change the precision of the machine. His love, if indeed he had love, was evidenced only in the perfection of the machine. One could conceivably thank him for having made the universe an orderly thing where sodium could not capriciously decide to be carbon, but that was all. We could not thank him for the forgiveness of our sins, for the simple reason that as small cogs in the machine we had no choice but to turn as the wheels turned. We had no sins to forgive.

For us of the Christian church, the one clue to God is Jesus Christ. He who was born in Bethlehem, suffered under Pontius Pilate, was crucified and rose again the third day— he it is who reveals the Father to us. But he is more than the revealer. He is God come within reach of man. He who is both the Son of Man and the Son of God, we have been bold to describe as "very God of very God." He is the Second Person of the Holy Trinity. Through him and in him we understand God to be the creating, judging, redeeming, justifying, reconciling God. He "so loved the world that He gave His only Son." This is the measure of God's love for man.

We will never know the love of God by contemplating the wonder of sunshine and rainfall. We will know his love only as we see him in the face of Jesus Christ, in the Christ who by his life, death, and resurrection made possible the forgiveness of our sins and our restoration to the Father.

The Biblical drama is the key to the understanding of man and his plight. Man is a creature of God, who is given the gift of independence, the right of choice. He disobeys God, and in his disobedience becomes captive to the enemy of God. The enemy brainwashes him, makes him love the darkness of the prison cell rather than the light of the Father's house. Man is estranged from God and from himself. Left to himself he would remain in bondage forever. But God, in his mercy, does not abandon him. In the fulness of time, God sent his Son to overcome the enemy, to set man free from his captivity, to forgive his sins and to usher him into the Kingdom of God, where he lives under the Lordship of the risen Lord.

Whatever new imagery modern man may need to supplement the imagery of earlier ages, the essential drama of God and man as given us in Scripture remains the core of the church's message in every age. God breaks through to us in Christ. His death and resurrection become the guarantee of God's love. The cross is the measure of man's sin and of God's mercy. In the event of Christ, God provides reconciliation for the world.

The absence of trust and the presence of anxiety is man's deepest offense

against a God who loves him with an everlasting love

5

The Grand Sinner

The dimension of man's sin is in direct ratio to his high station. If he is no more than a complex arrangement of protoplasm, he is no sinner at all. If he is a man among men only, engaged in a network of horizontal inter-personal relationships, his offenses are relative and indefinite. But if he is a child of God, created to the royalty of God's household, under obligation to live the life of holiness in God's family, then his disobedience becomes of colossal proportions. It was Absalom who rebelled against his father, the king. Had he been a peasant, it would have been but an incident; but it was a son who rebelled, and this shook the kingdom and broke the king's heart. If man were but a creature among all other creatures, his offenses need not be more than mischief. But he is a son of God, of the image of God, commissioned to have dominion over the earth and destined to live with God forever. He is a prince in the most royal of all houses, the house of God. His injustices against his fellow men are crimes against God. He is not a trivial offender. He is the grand sinner.

Man steals his existence from God. This is the supreme theft of all time. Man receives his existence from God and every moment of his life is dependent on God. He cannot keep his heart beating a single moment by willing it. Yet, totally dependent as he is, he embezzles his life from God. If he uses one talent as if it were his own to use as he pleases, if he lives one hour as if that hour were his, if he manages his property or money as if these were his, he then becomes a fraud, a pretender, a thief.

Man affronts God in unbelief. Luther's explanation of the first commandment, "We should fear, love and trust in God above all things," summarizes man's obligation to God. The most elemental of all obligations is trust or belief. Anxiety itself, which is really the absence of trust, is a cardinal sin. It is the sin that pierces the heart of God as a sword. As an earthly father I can overlook my child's burst of anger, I can easily forgive a petty theft, but if my child should conclude that I did not love him or that I was really not his father at all and he should, therefore, no longer come to me for anything or ever count on me for anything—in fact, should ignore me—this would be the greatest hurt of all. This absence of trust and presence of anxiety is man's deepest offense against a God who loves him with an everlasting love, and who went to the lengths of a cross to recover him and hold him.

It is only in relation to God that man attains the stature of a sinner. Over against his fellow men he is little more than a trouble maker; over against himself he is but a betrayer of his own humanity or integrity. It is as he stands before God, a son who has been assigned the management of the earth and who, despite his mismanagement is nonetheless reclaimed as a son—it is only then that man rises to such heights that his fidelity is divine and his infidelity is demonic. He is a prince, fallen and rebellious, whose sin is a rejection of God and a betrayal of existence itself.

Rejection of God is rejection of the brother. A man cannot be faithful to God and faithless to his brother. "As you did it to one of the least of these my brethren, you did it to me." The question of man's relation to man holds the center of the stage today. The most common focus of guilt, at least for Western man, is now his neglect of the brother. The sins of omission cry to heaven. "I was hungry (hundreds of millions are hungry the world over) and you gave me no food; I was a stranger (hundreds of millions have been made homeless in this turbulent century) and you did not welcome me." This sense of guilt over our neglect of the brother becomes monstrous when we recognize that we are sons of the One Father and that every neglect of the brother is a neglect of the Lord who died on a cross for all. It is when the horizontal dimension of our sin against the brother suddenly discloses itself in the vertical dimension of sin against God that sin takes on a cosmic, demonic stature. We are no trifling offenders; we are the grand sinners.

When forgiven man turns to praise his Lord he may thank him for health and peace and sunshine and rain, but the very heart of his LAUDAMUS will always be the forgiveness of sins.

The Gospel - Forgiveness

Where there is forgiveness of sins, there is life and salvation. This brief summary by Luther is the key to the spiritual life of the churches and the open door to all true worship.

Man is the blind one who needs light. He is the defeated one who needs victory. He is the bewildered one who needs meaning for life. Neither blindness nor bewilderment nor defeat describes his deepest plight and need, however. He is the disobedient one who needs forgiveness! He need feel no guilt over being blind or bewildered or defeated. He is guilty only if he is disobedient. Blind and bewildered and defeated as he is, he may rest

securely in the love of God. But as the disobedient one, he separates himself from God
and faces the judgment of God. Now he
needs redemption, reconciliation, forgiveness!

God entered the human scene in Christ
Jesus to forgive. This mighty act of redemption, climaxing in a cross and a resurrection,
gave the world the right to be reconciled to
God again.

When forgiven man turns to praise his
Lord, he may thank him for health and peace
and sunshine and rain, but the very heart of
his *laudamus* will always be the forgiveness
of sins which gives him the right to the Kingdom, through Christ, his Savior, Brother and
Lord.

It is when law and gospel are proclaimed
together as *the* Word of God to man that confession of sin becomes more than a jurid-
ical acknowledgment. Only against the back-
ground of God's immeasurable love in Christ
and the forgiveness of sin will man, out of a
broken heart, at once cry for mercy and
praise for mercy. Law without forgiveness
will elicit defiance; forgiveness without law
will elicit indifference. Law and Gospel,
joined in *One Word*, will yield repentance,

gratitude, freedom, peace, joy, and glad obedience. The traditional liturgies of the church
always contain both confession and forgiveness, often intertwined in such a way that it
is difficult to say that one clearly comes before the other. They are the *One Word* of
God to man. It is hardly no more than
academic to discuss the one (confession)
without the other (forgiveness).

It is one of the strange phenomena of our
time that just at the moment in history when
the secular world, through its writers of fiction, its dramatists, and its psychiatrists,
speaks more universally of the sense of guilt
than ever before—that just at this moment the
church speaks less of confession and forgiveness than before. We speak of the gap between man and man which needs to be
bridged by reconciliation. We speak of the
cleavage within man himself, which needs
healing by the discovery of identity. We dart
furtively here and there to find new and
relevant forms by which to address modern
man, while in the depths of his spirit he cries
out for forgiveness and for the reconciliation
and identity which only the forgiveness of
God can provide. When through the all-in-

clusive forgiveness of God man is accepted
by God, then he can accept himself (identity) and then he also can accept his brother
(reconciliation).

The message of God's forgiveness is the
most profound word given to man. It takes
man's plight with utter seriousness; it takes
the incredible dimensions of God's love with
utter seriousness. The orders of creation may
indeed speak of a gracious God, but it is in
the cross alone that God's love breaks through
with unmistakable brilliance. Here he forgives the sinner and returns him to the
brother, to himself, and to God. Alienation
and estrangement are gone. Man is at one
again, with God and with all creation.

The notable thing about man, even the
Christian man, is not that he is loving and
forgiving. He will always fall short in per-
formance. The noteworthy thing is that he is
the loved one, the forgiven one. This is the
word of the gospel. God takes the initiative to
love him and to forgive him. It is by God's
grace alone that he is restored. He is a son,
by grace through faith, and not because he
looks like a son, talks like a son, or performs
like a son. The only begotten Son has won the

right of sonship for him. Man's righteousness is the righteousness of Another. Man's favor with God is the favor given him by Jesus Christ, and Son of God and the Son of Man. Nothing in all the imaginations of man can shake him to his depths as can the staggering news that God receives him through grace, quite apart from any inventory of his own goodness. If this good news cannot reach him and win him, nothing can. God has risked everything on the gospel of forgiveness in Christ. Failing this, man is forever lost, separated from God, from himself and from his brothers.

The far country
with its husks and
pig sty
fade into forgetfulness.
We are the delivered
ones and we frolic
in the company of god.

7

The Style of Life

Forgiveness of sins will dictate a new and radical style of life. This is the life of the spirit within the church of Christ.

There will be a new and pervasive kind of gratitude. Anchored in a love which once and for all forgives all our sins and nestles us securely in the Father's care, our gratitude soars above the variants of life. We may be sick or well, rich or poor, living or dying—in all these circumstances the great gift of life with God remains unchanged. Nothing in all creation can separate us from the love of God in Christ Jesus. There are people like that, whose lives are a steady flow of thankfulness to God for His mercy, and who remain sweet and patient with their fellow men because of this surging gratitude to God.

There will be continuing repentance, a daily renewal, in which the drama of confession and forgiveness of sin and grace, of sorrow and joy, is the climate of life. It does not plunge into melancholy. It does not soar off into romanticism. It lives in the realism of daily sin on the one hand and the constancy of God's mercy on the other. It rests in *simul justus et peccator*. It faces squarely the gap between what a man ought to be and what he is, but knows that the gap is bridged by God's unfailing forgiveness. The sins, though scarlet, are white as snow.

There will be joy, the joy of being returned to the Father's house, where the Father prepares a feast, and there is singing and dancing. The earth is the Lord's, and we are the Lord's, and therefore the earth is ours again in a fresh stewardship. All is ours and our brothers' to enjoy. Everything now should give us increased pleasure: the splendor of the sunset, the laughter of a child, the winds caressing our hair. We are at home again with our Creator Father. The far country with its husks and pig sty fade into forgetfulness. We are the delivered ones, and we frolic in the company of God.

Hope returns. Man who had lost God and with God any hope for the morrow now faces the future with strange confidence. The threats of ungovernable technology no longer paralyze him nor send him into panic. The technology itself is God's gift for man to use. Moreover, God has not abandoned the planet. He who sent his Son to die for man and who with the Son sent the Holy Spirit to lead man into the truth and comfort him, certainly such a God can be counted on never to forsake a creature of such incalculable value. Whatever odds we face in the maelstrom of the world's problems, the unpredictable future is not out of God's hands. The earth may hold unsurpassed good for our grandchildren. With God nothing is impossible. Death itself, whether it comes to us one by one, trickling out of hospital beds, or whether it comes in catastrophic holocaust, death does not have the last word. For the Kingdom has an epic sweep which death cannot touch. There was a resurrection, there will be resurrections, and there will be the return of our Lord in glory.

And love becomes the rule of life. He who began the good work in us will move it on to perfection. Its perfection is love, for God is love. The kind of love that gives and gives and never demands *(agape)* has now been loosed among men. The Christ who dwells within us infects us with this same radical, unconditioned love. We turn to our brothers to claim them as brothers, not because they are attractive, not even because they want us, but because we, like our Lord, cannot do less. We love because he first loved us. And he whom we seek to serve in love opens only one door. We serve him by serving our brothers. We serve them one by one as they cross our path or as we seek them out. We serve them corporately by assuming responsibility for all the created orders of life. The earth is the Lord's, and therefore everything on it is his: governments, industries, schools, homes, transportation, communication. The cause of justice and truth, peace and production, become our cause in our service of the brother.

THE AUTHOR

Alvin N. Rogness has been president of Luther Theological Seminary St. Paul, Minn., since 1954. He served pastorates at Duluth, Minn., Ames and Mason City, Iowa, and Sioux Falls, S.D.

Dr. Rogness, the author of seven books, has twice participated in the Protestant Religion Missions sponsored by the U.S. Air Force in Europe and has conducted chaplains' retreats in Japan. He has served as a member of various Lutheran World Federation Committees including the Commission on Worship and Spiritual Life.